Aquaponics 101

An Introduction To Backyard Aquaponic Gardening

TABLE OF CONTENTS

Introduction

Thank you for purchasing the book, "Aquaponics 101: An Introduction To Backyard Aquaponic Gardening".

This book contains various strategies for setting up an aquaponic garden in your own backyard.

In today's world, most of the foods that people eat run a high risk of containing toxic chemicals. These chemicals can come from various sources. It all starts with how the food is grown.

Massive amounts of fertilizers, pesticides, antibiotics, growth enhancers and insecticides are applied to the plants from seed germination to harvest. After harvesting, these crops are again subjected to a barrage of chemicals to preserve their quality during transport to various outlets like markets, groceries, restaurants and food manufacturers. By the time it is served, food is already a cocktail of chemicals.

Because of the health risks from these chemicals, people are increasingly leaning towards eating organic foods or foods that have not been exposed to any chemicals. However, the certification of organic foods is also unreliable.

To ensure that you are getting healthy, nutritious, and 100% organic foods, grow them through aquaponics. With this food growing method, there is no room for harmful additives. No gardener can add any toxic chemicals in the system and get away with it.

Aquaponics is a purely organic, natural way of growing food, which employs the natural mutually beneficial relationship between plants and animals.

In this book, you will learn all about aquaponics and how to set up your own aquaponics garden with the help of some easy-to-follow steps.

You have been given the entire process in the first chapter. It has been simplified to help you understand what steps you will have to take to ensure that you have the best aquaponics system in the neighborhood. You have also been given tips and tricks that you can use when your system is up and running.

Most gardeners forget that their plants have to be taken care of too. When you look at an aquaponics system, you will have to cater to the needs of each individual entity of the system. You cannot forget about one part to take care of another. Ensure that you take care of the fish and the plants equally.

Thanks again for purchasing this book, I hope you enjoy it!

Mickey

Chapter 1:

What is Aquaponics?

Concepts of Aquaponics Gardening

One of the oldest forms of plant cultivation and fish raising is aquaponics. This is a method that combines aquaculture (raising fishes) and hydroponics (growing plants). Aquaponics basically takes all the positive aspects of aquaculture and hydroponics and eliminates the negative ones. For instance, in hydroponics, expensive nutrients are needed to feed the plants. The systems also need periodic flushing due to generated wastes. In aquaculture, periodic flushing is also required due to the buildup of ammonia-rich waste that can pollute the water and kill the fish residing within. Aquaponics eliminates the need for periodic flushing, expensive food, and issues regarding waste disposal. In fact, the waste from aquaculture is already nitrogen-rich, which is an excellent alternative to expensive food for the plants. And because plants use fish waste as food, the water in the system is naturally cleansed, thus eliminating the need for periodic flushing. Also, water between the plants and fishes can be circulated. Wastewater from the fish goes into the plant tank, where it is considered as food. Cleansed water is returned to the fish tank, already rich in oxygen from plant photosynthesis.

BENEFITS

A lot of people prefer to grow food, using aquaponics. One of the major issues that aquaponics addresses, is the issue of food safety. Most people prefer eating organic foods, but certification is not always reliable. Often, once an inspector certifies a farm or food producer of being organic, there is rarely any follow-up to assure that organic foods continue to be produced. There is risk that once the certification is obtained, manufacturer and food producers may no longer follow strict organic farming and growing methods. One likely indication for this is the huge discrepancy between actual organically grown foods and "organic" foods sold in the market. More foods are being sold as organic compared to the actual number of produce from organic growers.

With aquaponics, cheating is not possible. Growers cannot use any pesticide and other harmful chemicals anywhere in the aquaponics system. This is because fishes are very sensitive to pollutants. Even the smallest concentration of toxic chemicals can kill the fishes. That includes "organically-approved" pesticides. These pesticides, even with a certification of being organic, are still toxic and can kill the fishes. Hence, an aquaponics system is purely organic; no chemicals are used either on the plants or the fishes.

The basic fact is that aquaponics does not need any synthetic chemicals anywhere in the system. It already mimics that mutually beneficial relationship between plants and animals that occurs naturally. Fertilizers needed to boost plant production are already provided by fishes. Fertilizers used on plants in other farming methods are rich in ammonia. This compound is naturally found in fish waste. Fishes thrive well in clean and unpolluted waters. Water cleaning and filtering is naturally performed by the plants.

Other Benefits

Farming

One of the many benefits that can be obtained is better farming techniques. There is more harvest compared to traditional soil farming. In fact, some growers report reaping up to 6 times more produce per square foot of planted area compared to soil farming.

Traditional soil farming wastes a lot of water. Much of the water in soil farming goes into the ground; only a small percentage is eventually absorbed by the plant roots. In aquaponics, it may seem that there is a lot of water used. Imagine two tanks filled with water. However, the water is being recirculated, and not much leaves the system. In fact, aquaponics uses 90% less water compared to water usage in traditional farming methods. Because of this same reason, aquaponics is the best farming method to use during droughts or in places where water is scarce.

There is also no weeding since plants are grown in well-controlled media. Plants grow almost two times faster compared to those planted in soil. This is because of the continuous rich supply of nitrogen from fish excrement. This means cashing in on the crops earlier, with more earnings because of less labor, fewer expenses (e.g. no fertilizer purchases, etc.) and higher yields. Aside from that, depending on the type of fish raised, income can also come from the sale of these fishes.

Environment

Fertilizers carry toxic chemicals that can mix with the soil, seep into the groundwater, and pollute bodies of water through runoff. Traditional farming uses fertilizers in an attempt to augment the nutrients in the soil. There is no need for additional fertilizers with aquaponics because the nutrients are regularly replenished. In fact, as long as the fishes are alive, there is a continuous supply of plant food.

Land conservation is also a benefit of aquaponics. Less space is needed to produce up to 6 times more crops within the same space compared to conventional farming.

Health

Most organic fertilizers come from animal sources. These bring risks of carrying pathogens such as Salmonella and E. coli. Eating vegetables grown with these fertilizers may transmit diseases such as food poisoning and gastroenteritis.

Fishes raised in aquaponics systems are certified free of mercury contamination (compared to some wild caught fishes that thrive in mercuryladen areas of the oceans and sea), no hormones (which can kill plants if added to the system, hence a no-no), no antibiotics (which can also kill off the plants) and no PCBs.

Applications of the aquaponics system

This section explains to you some of the major forms of the aquaponics system as witnessed all around the world. This is a basic list; there are other applications as well!

Small scale or domestic aquaponics system

You may have an aquaponics system that is the size of close to a thousand liters. It may have a growing space of three-meters squared. This is considered to be a domestic or a small-scale aquaponics system. It is perfect for the production of food for a household. This system has been tried and tested in various corners of the world. It has proved to be a success. The main purpose of this system is to provide nutrition to a household. They help in sustaining the household since the system has different units that produce fruits and vegetables as and when required. The best application of this type of an aquaponics system is to provide sustenance and nutrition to a household.

Commercial and Semi – commercial Aquaponics Systems

There are very few commercial and semi – commercial aquaponics systems across the world. This is because of the high cost that people have to incur during the construction of the system. There are a lot of commercial systems that have been dropped since the profits that have been obtained from these systems did not meet the initial cost. Most of these systems do not exist where people practice the monoculture of plants, especially the production of basil or lettuce. There are universities that have conducted experiments on the large aquaponics systems, but these are only for academic purposes. They were not designed to produce any food as such.

How the system works

There are five simple steps that have to be undertaken to ensure that the system works well. This section covers these systems.

Step 1

You have to ensure that the tanks that you have in the system are perfect for raising fish. This is the first step. You will have to ensure that the fish in the aquaponics system are growing just fine. You have to ensure that the water content and the nutrients in the tanks are perfect for the fish.

Step 2

The next step is to pump the water towards the plants. The water in the tank has to be sent to the plants so that the roots of the plants can ensure that the required amount of nutrients are flowing through the plant and are making the plants stronger. This will ensure that they do not wither away or dry up. You will need to ensure that the amount of nutrients in the water is perfect for the plants. Ensure that there is enough calcium, potassium and iron in the water.

Step 3

There will be certain ammonium products that have been produced by the fish. The fish are fed on a regular basis. The waste that the fish produce contains the required nutrients. The ammonium content in the water increases whenever there is an accumulated waste. This is removed by the nitrifying bacteria. They convert the ammonium compounds into nitrate ions that help in the growth of the plants.

Step 4

Once the nutrients have been released into the water, the roots of the plants absorb the nutrients that are required by the plant. You have to ensure that there are no blockages in your pipes. This will be covered in detail in the latter chapters. If there is any sort of blockage, you will find that the flow of nutrients has been stunted resulting in the stunted growth of the plants.

Step 5

Your system has a filter that cleans up the entire water that has been passing through the system. You will not have to waste any extra water by refilling the fish tanks. The filter in your system filters the water and sends it back to the fish rearing tanks to help the fish survive.

Chapter 2:

The Types of Aquaponics Systems

There are many different types of systems used in setting up an aquaponics garden. Some of the most common ones used by a lot of backyard gardeners are media-filled beds, NFT (nutrient film technique), and DWC (deep water culture).

Media Filled Beds

These are the simplest and most common aquaponics systems. Containers are cleaned and filled with rock medium, such as expanded clay and other similar materials. Plants are grown in this kind of medium. A pump is used to bring water from the tank where fishes are raised to the media filled beds. Water either runs in a continuous flow over the rocks or floods the media beds, which are then drained at a later time.

For systems using the flood drain cycles, it can be achieved through several means. There are 3 main methods through which this cycle can be achieved using a timed pump, using an auto-siphon and using a simple standpipe.

Some media-filled bed systems use a timer. It sets when to flood the beds with water from the fish tank by turning on the pump and when to drain it by turning off the pump. A standpipe is placed in the grow beds to control flooding levels.

Flooding and draining the grow beds can also be performed through the use of an auto siphon

Placed within the beds and the pump is allowed to run continuously. The siphon would periodically drain off the water from the grow beds and return them into the fish tank.

A standpipe in the bed and a continuously running pump is also one way to flood and drain.

Pros and Cons

This section covers the pros and cons of this method of aquaponics.

Pros

- This system works great for people who have taken up aquaponics as a hobby.

- You will find that the parts for the system are easily found. They do not cost too much either. You will be able to procure the material with ease.

- The size of the system depends on your interest. You can make it a big system or a small system. You will be able to save on a lot of space using this method.

- You will be able to grow different kinds of plants.

-

Cons

- This system will have to be cleaned on a regular basis

- There may be areas in the entire system, which have become anaerobic.

Nutrient Film Technique (NFT)

This technique is more commonly used in hydroponics but also works well in aquaponics. In NFT, water filled with nutrients (from the fish tanks) is pumped into the plants through small gutters. These gutters are enclosed and the water flows through it in very thin films. The plants are in small plastic cups and their roots are allowed access to the thin films of water for nutrient absorption.

This technique is only recommended for certain plants. Plants like leafy greens would thrive well with NFT. Plants too large for plastic cups and with large and invasive root systems are not recommended for this system. Plants that grow too heavy to hang in plastic cups are also not for the NFT.

Pros and Cons

This section covers the pros and cons of this method of aquaponics.

Pros

-       The materials in this system are readily available. You will find the parts for this system in the market with ease.

-       The growing conditions for this system are more precise. You will be able to select your plants with ease.

-       You will find that you are able to change the media without having to worry about a change in the pH of the water. A change in the pH would prove to be extremely dangerous for the plants in the system.

Cons

-       You will have to filter the water on a regular basis. This needs to be done well. You will find that the fish have died otherwise.

-       You cannot have a lot of crops growing in this system. This is because of the conditions that have been set by the system.

Deep Water Culture

This type of system works by floating the plants on the surface and the roots dangle into the water. This is among the more commonly practiced aquaponics technique used for commercial growing. There are various ways to achieve this. Some growers place the plants on foam rafts and allow them to float across a tank continuously filled with water from the fish tank. The water is cycled continuously up to the plants and down into the fish tank.

Chift Pist System

This is one of the most popular DIY aquaponics systems. A sump tank houses water, which is pumped into the tank where the fishes are. As the water is pumped into the fish tank, the water level rises until it overflows. The excess water flows out of the tank and into the grow beds. Water that gets into the grow beds eventually drains off back into the sump tank. An auto-siphon is placed within the grow bed to control the flooding and draining.

Often, growers incorporate an SLO for the chift pist system. An SLO is Solids Lift Overflow. An overflow pipe is installed into the fish tank, which goes down into the base of the fish tank. This will draw up all solids (i.e., fish waste) that settles down at the bottom and draw it up into the grow beds.

There are many advantages to this system. One benefit is that the pump is situated away from the wastes and the fishes. It is located in the sump tank. This way, the pump is able to perform better without disturbing the fishes and agitating the wastes, which can cloud the water. Also, this system allows for consistency in the water level of the fish tank, which lessens the stress on the fishes. This is also the most recommended for tall fish tanks as it makes water circulation and waste removal more efficient.

There are also some downsides to using the chift pist system. There is the need to install additional equipment, which is the sump tank. Also, in order for this to work well, the fish tank or stand should be tall. Also, this system would require a larger area to house the entire setup. Timers are also not possible to use for this system.

Aquaponics systems can be as simple or as complex as the grower prefers. The simplest to start with, especially for those who do not wish to purchase equipment is to set up a regular aquarium. Take a few pieces of polystyrene. Cut a few small holes in it. Insert cuttings of plants like watercress and mint into these holes. Float the polystyrene on the surface o the aquarium water. Place fishes and in an instant, a simple aquaponics system.

Based on years of research and feedback, most aquaponics gardeners consider the flood and drain system as the simplest yet the most reliable of all systems. This system requires a very minimal amount of work for care and maintenance. This is also the most recommended system for beginners.

Chapter 3:

Basic Tools and Equipment

To start setting up an aquaponics garden, you should consider a few things. Think of the purpose of the garden. Is it for commercial growing (i.e., sell the crops to local markets) or is it for household consumption or just to grow ornamental plants? Next, decide what system to use, where to place the aquaponics setup, and how large each component will be. Then, gather the supplies and equipment.

Materials to use

Fish tank

The material to house the fishes can be made of plastic, rubber, plexiglass or glass. In fact, any container that can hold water can be used. Examples include a barrel, bucket or plastic tub. It should be large enough to hold anywhere between 3 and 20 gallons of water. If there is enough space, a much larger container may be used.

A larger fish tank can support a larger grow bed. About 10 gallons of water in the fish tank can support 1 to 2 square feet of growing area.

Make sure that the containers are clean and free of residual chemicals. Recycled containers can be used but avoid using those that once contained toxic chemicals, petroleum products, and other harmful compounds. Clean the containers well before using.

Gravel

This will be placed at the bottom of the plant tank. This is where the nitrifying bacteria will settle. The bacteria are crucial in converting ammonia from fish waste into nitrites. Plants use nitrates as food in order to grow fast and healthy.

Gravel can be bought in pet stores, in natural or artificial colors. The size of each pebble is about one-eighth of an inch.

Wash the gravel before placing in the tank. Dust and dirt may be present, which can cloud tank

Water and add pollutants.

Water tubing and pump

A water pump is required to bring water from the fish tank up into the grow beds. A small one is often enough for this purpose. On the other hand, a larger and more complicated aquaponics setup may require a larger and heavy-duty type of water pump.

There should be enough tubing for water going up to the grow beds. Tubing for water draining back into the fish tank is optional, depending on the type of system used. Make sure the lengths are adequate. Tubing should be long enough to reach the grow beds but not too long that the tube forms loops along its length. To measure the tubing, it should run from the pump outlet and reach into the grow bed and a few extra length to encircle the beds.

Air stone, pump and tubing

An air pump is also important, especially for large setups and if there are lots of fishes in the tank. Oxygen is crucial for fishes to thrive. In hot weather, there is less oxygen dissolved in the water, which can spell trouble for the fishes. Augment oxygen in the water by placing an air pump setup. Place the air stone at the bottom of the tank. Connect it to tubing and attach the tubing to the air pump, which is placed a little above and away from the fish tank. The function of the air stone is to break the air into smaller bubbles, making it easier to dissolve in the water.

Grow bed

This is where the plant will be placed and grown. The grow bed-sits at the topmost portion of the tank. This should be slightly wider and longer than the tank. Growing medium is added to the beds.

As with the fish tank, any container that can adequately and properly house the plants can be used. A plastic container or garden planter may do. One can also have a grow bed specially built out of plexiglass. Use only non-toxic silicon glue for this kind of grow bed. Just make sure that the grow bed is not too heavy that it can damage the tank or too unstable that it will topple off.

Whatever the kind of container used, it should be 3 inches to 8 inches deep.

Growing medium

These are chemically inert and porous materials that are placed in the growing beds. The purpose of these is to hold the roots and to maintain moisture. Commonly used growing media include peat moss, perlite, pea gravel, coconut coir and expanded clay pebbles. Place enough of any or combination of these materials to fill the grow beds.

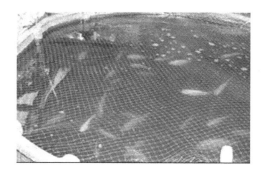

Fish and Plants

These are the most important living components of the aquaponics system. There are several kinds that a grower can choose from, depending on preference and purpose.

Optional additions to an aquaponics setup:

Aquarium heater

This is optional equipment added to the aquaponics system. Ornamental tropical fishes will certainly thrive well with a heater, especially is the aquaponics is in a colder region. Tropical fishes require 78°F tan temperature in order to thrive well.

Growers can choose from 2 types of aquarium heaters. There is a submerged type and a tank side mounted one. The sizes vary, too. Choose one that can adequately heat up the fish tank.

Aquarium Lights

These are placed in the fish tank to provide good lighting for monitoring the health of the fishes.

Growth Lights for the plants

If the system is set up in an area that receives low light or is often exposed to only brief periods of sunlight, placing grow lights is a good option. Plants need light in order to grow vigorous and healthy. However, bright lights can also encourage algae growth in the fish tank. When using growth lights, make sure that the lights do not directly shine on the fish tank. Grow lights are not necessary if the grow beds are already receiving ample amounts of sunlight such as when situated near a window with streaming bright sunlight, in a greenhouse or the plant naturally does not require lots of sunlight for growth.

Chapter 4:

The Ten Guidelines for Aquaponics Systems

It is essential that these guidelines are followed. They are not ranked in the order of their importance since they are all crucial!

Feeding Rate Ratio for design calculations

When you are designing and planning your aquaponics system, you will have to ensure that the ratio between your fish and the plants is based on the feeding rate ratio. This ratio is based on how much food is fed to the fish per square meter area of land where the plants are grown. This ratio is calculated on a regular basis. If you have the raft hydroponic system, you will have to ensure that the feeding rate ratio varies from 60 to 100 grams per meter square per day. For instance, if you have been feeding the fish close to 2000 grams a day, you will need to ensure that the plants in your backyard cover at least an area of 32 meter square to ensure that the feeding rate ratio is between the optimum range. This is the same even when looked at conversely. The optimum or correct feeding rate ratio depends on certain factors – the type of system you are using for the aquaponics system in your backyard, the different kinds of plants that you are cultivating, the composition of chemicals in the water source and also the amount of water that you lose when you are removing any solids from the water.

The Feed input must be constant

This is an extremely important aspect that you must keep in mind. There are two methods that you can use to ensure that the amount of food you give your fish remains constant.

Multiple fish rearing tanks

This is the first method that can be used. You will also have to ensure that you have staggered production. One such system that can be used is the UVI aquaponics system. This system uses four fish rearing tanks. These tanks are tilapia tanks. They require a minimum production cycle of 24 weeks. The tilapia in each of these tanks is all at different stages of growth. Due to this difference, they can be harvested at different times, sometimes at six weeks too! When this tilapia is harvested, the feed input decreases by 25 – 30% and then increases over the next six weeks. Although the levels fluctuate, the feed input often remains constant. When the tanks are being stocked with the fresh tilapia, the level of nutrients is low. However, as the tanks are being harvested, the nutrient level is high. This results in very poor plant growth.

One Fish Rearing tank with Different sizes of fish

Let us take an example of the Tilapia and fish that have a grow–out period of six months. This would imply that the tank has six different sizes of fish. These fish have been grouped into different categories. Every month, a grader bar will be used to pull out the largest fish from the tank. When you remove the largest fish, you will have to restock the tank with the baby tilapia, also called the fingerling. This has to be done after every harvest. This will, however, change the feeding rate. It will fluctuate over every harvesting period. The advantage of this system is that it reduces the amount of space used and does not require extravagant expenditure. There are two major disadvantages of this system:

1. Since the fish are removed using the grader bar, it reduces their mortality.

2. If there are fish that have been hurt or have a slow growth, they will have escape being captured. They will also use up a lot of the food that have been inserted into the system.

Use Potassium, Iron and Calcium as substitutes

Every plant requires thirteen nutrients to ensure a good growth. The fish feed that is inserted into the system provides the plants with ten of those nutrients. But, the problem with the feed is that the levels of potassium, iron and calcium are extremely low. To ensure that the levels do not affect the growth of plants, they need to be supplemented. Consider the UVI aquaponics system. In this system, calcium and potassium are provided in the form of supplements to the plants. They are inserted as basic compounds to adjust the pH. Iron is also added as a supplement. It is added as a chelated compound where iron is attached to an organic structure that ensures that the nutrient does not precipitate form the solution.

There has to be good Aeration

Every animal and plant requires a good amount of oxygen. When you have an aquaponics system, you have to ensure that the system provides good amounts of oxygen for the fish, the plants, and the bacteria. The oxygen is often provided through dissolved oxygen. The levels of this dissolved oxygen should range between 5 to 10 milligrams per liter. This has to be maintained in the fish rearing tanks and in the water that surrounds the roots of the plants that are being cultivated. It is important to ensure that an adequate amount of dissolved oxygen is maintained to have healthy populations of nitrifying bacteria. These bacteria are required since they convert toxic levels of ammonia and nitrite to relatively low and non–toxic ions of nitrogen. The ammonia is often secreted by the fish into the tanks through their gills. The dissolved oxygen is required to ensure that this ammonia is converted into non–toxic levels of nitrogen. This process is called nitrification.

Remove Solids

You may provide 100 grams of fish feed to the fish in the tanks. Close to 25 grams of this feed are excreted as solid waste into the tank. This is often based on dry weight. But when it comes to the weight of the solids in the water, it is greater than their dry weight. Hence, it is essential to remove this solid waste from the tanks as frequently as possible. This waste always passes through the flow stem. It can be removed through filtering or through settling the waste before it passes through the flow stem. If these solids are not removed from the tanks, they will stunt the growth of the plants. The level of oxygen in the entire system will decrease. The roots will begin to decay and start affecting the soil. These solids have an adverse effect on the nitrifying bacteria. It is important that these solids are removed. They form excess amounts of ammonia and use up all the oxygen that is available in the tanks.

Be wary of Aggregates

You find different aggregates in your system on a regular basis. Pea gravel, perlite, and sand are excellent examples of the media that are used to grow plants in various aquaponics systems. There is solid matter that is frequently generated in these systems. This solid media often clogs the different pipes and will channelize the flow of water. Since there are certain areas that have been clogged, they will ensure that the water does not flow through them. When the water flow is inhibited, the areas become anaerobic, that is they become areas that have no oxygen in them. This inevitably causes the death of the plants in the system. If you remove particulate organic matter from the water, you will find that there is enough dissolved oxygen in the water that will promote the growth of the plants and the nitrifying bacteria. There are other organisms that are required to ensure that the plants grow well. The removal of solid parts ensures that these organisms grow freely. At times, there are certain bacteria, either living or dead, that will become aggregates. If you would like to use this aggregate media, you can use it as a substitute for fish feed. This would mean that you reduce the rate at which you stock the fish in the tanks.

Have oversized pipes

This seems funny does it not? After having said that you have to minimize the space used and also try to minimize the waste, why would you have to use large pipes instead of small ones?

Oversized pipes are often used to reduce the negative effects of bio –fouling. You will find that the same principle that is used when it comes to aggregates is used for the pipes. You will find that when there is a high level of organic matter that has been dissolved in the water, there will be a rapid growth of filamentous bacteria, which will restrict the flow of water in the pipes. This restriction leads to very low amounts of oxygen produced in these areas in the system. If you have thin tubes, you will find that they are clogged often and sometimes have no water flowing through them. You could have pipes that are four inches thick. These too restrict the flow of water, partially in most cases, when there is bio – fouling. This causes the level of water in the rearing tanks to rise to great levels. In the UVI system, there are a few tilapia near the pipes that act as filters. They keep the drain lines free and remove the bio – fouling just by swimming through the pipes. They also graze on the filamental bacteria thereby reducing a number of such bacteria in the tank. When you have the pipes far away from the solid removal systems, you can ensure that the pipes are never clogged. This will ensure that the plants grow very well. Another point to remember is that if you have lower temperatures, you can ensure that the amount of bio – fouling decreases drastically reducing clogging. You will also have the opportunity to clean the tanks and the pipes occasionally instead of having to do it on a regular basis.

Ensure that you use Biological Control

You may choose to use pesticides to control the number of insects and pests in the aquaponics systems. This is a common practice. However, this must not be done. These pesticides are toxic to fish and will kill most of the different species that you may have in the tanks. There are certain medicines that are used to kill the parasites that harm the fish. They cannot be used in the tanks since they harm the bacteria that are found in the tanks. If vegetables are used, they will absorb the bacteria. Therefore, only biological methods have to be adopted when it comes to getting rid of parasites. It has been found that most scientists are looking at identifying new biological methods to ensure that aquaponics systems are able to sustain even without the use of pesticides. Most systems use the fish species like tilapia. This species ensures that the other fish in the tanks are not harmed by any diseasecausing parasites.

Adequate Biofiltration has to be done

You have removed all the solids that will harm the system. What do you think has to be done next? The nitrifying bacteria in your aquaponics system work on the oxidation of the ammonia produced to form nitrate ions, which will help in the growth of plants and also help in the sustenance of the system. If you ensure that the optimum feeding rate ratio is maintained in the system, you will be able to ensure that the water is treated very effectively without any external applications. There are certain aquaponics systems that use nutrient films. They have less of a surface area for the hydroponic components resulting in a smaller area for the nitrifying bacteria. Therefore, a biofilter is needed in these systems. These filters are also used in different aquaponics systems that have fish that require excellent quality of the water they live in. They are safer when compared with the tilapia. They also are less hardy.

Control the pH in the water

The pH is an extremely important entity. It is called the master variable. This controls different qualities of the variables in the entire aquaponics system. This is a key variable that ensures that the process of nitrification happens with ease. When the pH lies between 7.5 and any value higher, nitrification happens with ease. However, when the pH falls to a 6, the process of nitrification dies slowly. You have to measure the pH on a regular basis, preferably daily. It has been found that for the process of nitrification, the pH must lie between a value that is either 6.5 or higher. It is best to have a pH of 7 in the aquaponics system since that ensures that there is a balance between the process of nitrification and nutrient solubility. If the pH is too high, you will find the effect in your plants. They begin to show a deficiency in nutrients and also have a stunted growth. If there is very low pH, the ammonia content accumulates to a very high level and proves toxic to the fish in the water. Therefore, it is important that the level of pH is maintained and monitored regularly.

There was once a wise man who said that he could design an aquaculture in his backyard using just one pump. That man was Dean Farrell. He had a farm that had a few hundred thousand pounds of the fish species tilapia and only used a pump that was 13 – hp. You must also try to ensure that you use one pump in your aquaponics system. Use this pump-to-pump water from the lowest point in the system to the highest point in the system. You should use gravity to let the water flow through the entire system. This rule saves a lot of money and also saves the level of aggregation.

Chapter 5:

The Advantages and the Disadvantages of an Aquaponics System

Throughout the book, you will come across the different advantages and disadvantages of an aquaponics system. This chapter provides some additional detail on the same. There is enough evidence to back these claimed advantages and disadvantages. These are often related to backyard aquaponics systems instead of the commercial aquaponics systems.

Advantages

This section covers the advantages that every backyard aquaponics system provides.

Reduction in water use

There is a significant reduction in the amount of water that is used throughout the system. It has been found that all the water is recycled through the system. You will not have to discard the water or change it when there is no disease-causing parasite in the water. It has been seen that the amount of water used in the aquaponics system is close to 90% lower than the water used in regular agriculture or soil gardening. If you have a tank that is filled with water around six weeks ago, you will find that the water level has decreased only by about 10 – 20%. This implies that you will only have to use 2 – 3 liters of water in the tank per day! This is very less when compared to traditional soil gardening.

Rapid growth of plants

You will find that the plants grow considerably faster in aquaponics systems when compared to traditional soil gardening. There has been no documented proof for the same. However, you can use the technique of aquaponics systems in your backyard and find the difference yourself. There is a good amount of nitrogen in the soil, which acts as a catalyst when cultivating plants. In the aquaponics systems, the plants have continuous access to nitrogen, which helps in increasing the speed of their growth. Soil gardens can be set up where the nutrients and water levels are maintained. This, however, does not have to be done in an aquaponics system. There are certain plants that grow better in an aquaponics system.

Healthier fruits and vegetables

It has been found that there are certain vegetables and plants that grow better in the aquaponics system when compared to traditional soil gardens. These vegetables and fruits look vibrant, healthy, big and full! These can be produced in regular soil gardens, but they take time.

No artificial fertilizers

In an aquaponics system, you do not require any additional fertilizers to feed your plants. There are certain systems that require you to add supplements for calcium, potassium, and iron. This is due to the fact that the feed used to provide nutrition to the fish have a low content of these nutrients. These fertilizers cannot be used since they would either kill or harm the fish in the tanks. You are saving costs and also resorting to an eco – friendly system. You would also not need any fertilizers to improve the condition of the soil before, during or after sowing the seeds or during the growth of the plant.

Year - round use

This system can be used to grow plants that can be used around the year. This cannot be done in the traditional soil gardening. Traditional soil gardening permits the use of grow beds which result in a green – house type of method for the growth of plants. This differentiation can be seen in cold areas since the temperature of the ground can be used to monitor the temperature of the tanks. This results in ensuring that the plants grow efficiently in the aquaponics system.

Reduced Pest damage

This is a known fact. When you have an aquaponics system, you will find that the leaves on the plants are less damaged when compared to the leaves on the plants that you have gardened in the soil. There are issues with the aquaponics system when it comes to pests. These can be overcome by using bio - fertilizers or the bioproducts that have been created. There may be some damage that has been caused to the plants. This minimal damage is acceptable. You do not lose an entire crop due to a pest in an aquaponics system.

You do not have to weed!

I am sure most of the gardeners out there are breathing a sigh of relief. Yes! You do not have to spend time crouching in your backyard and pulling weeds out! There are many different designs that can be used for the aquaponics system in your backyard. It has been seen that there are no weeds that grow in the aquaponics systems. The system is self – sustained. The system waters itself and provides a great environment for both the fish and the plants to sustain in. The fish and plants are able to grow with ease in this system. There is an occasional clean up that you will have to do to maintain the fish rearing tanks in the system. You will also have to clean the pumps and the pipes to ensure that the flow of water throughout the system is smooth and easy.

Disadvantages

There will always be certain disadvantages in the system along with the advantages. This does not mean that the system cannot be used. You can always find a way to work around the disadvantages when you know what they are.

Expensive

It has been claimed that this system is generally expensive to set up. The aquaponics systems require pumps, tubes, tanks, beds and the fish! These can be expensive depending on where you bring them. If you want to have the best quality, you may have to shell out more than you had initially planned on doing. You can be assured that a tiny backyard aquaponics system will not cost more than 2000 dollars. But when you want a large aquaponics system you may have to shell out an amount between 5000 and 10000 dollars. If you can devote some of your time and some of your energy, you will not have to spend that much on constructing the system. You may be able to reduce the cost by 25 – 50%! You will find that you can obtain grow beds and fish tanks for free. You can always get the gravel and sand from a river nearby or from your driveway. You will have to purchase the pumps and the power supplies though!

You may need a greenhouse

This is not true for every aquaponics system. There are certain regions that require a greenhouse to be installed before the system is set up. This always depends on the climate where the aquaponics system is being set up in. A greenhouse will protect the plants in the system from extensive heat and will also be able to prevent them from being attacked by pests. This is the same for the traditional soil gardening.

A good amount of knowledge

It is obvious that you will need to have a good amount of knowledge when you are going to set up your aquaponics system. There is a possibility that you may make mistakes while setting the system up. There are certain people who without their knowledge of the aquaponics systems have lost fish and have given up on the entire system. There is some knowledge required to ensure that the bacteria in the system is good for the system. The person setting up the system must have a good amount of knowledge on whether or not the ratio of water to food to fish is the correct amount for the system. You will also need to have enough knowledge on what plants to grow and what their requirements are.

Continuous monitoring of water

Although the amount of water used or wasted is not as large as the amount wasted in traditional soil gardening, you have to check the quality of the water on a regular basis. You will have to ensure that the water is suitable for the fish and the pH level is not too high or too low. This only has to be done in the first few months since you do not have an idea on the quality of water required. When your system has matured, you do not have to check the water more than once a week.

Electricity for the pumps

Traditional soil gardening requires no electricity but requires a lot of hard work on your part. With aquaponics gardening, you do not have to put in too much effort. However, you will need to have a source of electricity. You will have to ensure that the water pump works. If you have a system with aeration pumps, you will need to provide electricity for those too. You may have to run the pump for over three hours a day. Your electricity bill may increase. But if you have one pump to use for the system, you will not have to pay too much for the electricity. You have to optimize the flood and the drain cycles. Otherwise, you may have too much water at the roots of your plants resulting in drowning them.

Fish food!

You may not need to buy fertilizer and remember to use it every single day! But you have to do so with the fish food! Yes, you do. This seems very silly does it not? But it is only when you have fed your fish that your plants will grow. The fish gorge on the fish food and produce waste. This waste is used by the plants to grow. The waste contains nutrients that help in the growth of the plants! Fish are the best organisms that convert nay food into body mass. Hence, people use fish to procure proteins and other nutrients. You may choose to buy fish food from outside or plant duckweed or grow worms!

Chapter 6:

How to Set Up an Aquaponics Garden in the Backyard

Once all the equipment is gathered and ready, it's time to set up the aquaponics system. Follow these easy steps to set up a simple flood and drain aquaponics system:

1. **Clean the fish water and make sure there are no soap or chemical residues, especially when using recycled containers.**

2. Wash the gravel well and arrange it evenly on the bottom of a cleaned fish tank.

3. Take the grow bed and a drill. Bore holes about one-eighth to three-sixteenth of an inch for every 2 inches on the grow bed. These holes would be where water would drain out of the grow bed.

4. Choose one of the grow bed's back corners where the water pump tubing will go. Drill a hole with half an inch diameter.

5. Affix the water pump into the fish tank. Then, carefully place the grow bed above the tank.

6. Attach the water tubing to the pump and thread it through the ½-inch hole in the back corner of the grow

bed. Pull the tubing through the hole. The length should extend to about ¾ the height of the grow bed and then loop around the interior or the grow bed. Any excess should be cut off to avoid any loops and kinks. Fold over the end of the tube and tape securely with electrical tape.

7. Take the chosen growing medium and fill the grow bed with it. Place enough of the medium to reach the level of the tube.

8. For every 2 inches of the looped tube inside the grow bed, punch small holes.

9. Add more of the growing medium, about an inch or two to cover the loop of tube.

10. Slowly and carefully fill the fish tank with water. Plug the water pump into an electrical source to check for proper water flow. The water should be pumped up into the grow beds, which then seeps down through the layer of growing medium and flows right back into the fish tank. Adjust the flow to have a good water circulation without overflooding the grow bed.

11. Connect the air stone to one end of the tubing and the other end to the air pump. Submerge the air stone into the fish tank. Plug the air pump into an electrical source. A steady stream of micro-bubbles should come out of the air stone. This will provide fresh air to the water.

12. Get a litmus paper and check the pH of the water in the fish tank. This is the least expensive test kits

To check water pH. For an aquaponics system, the optimum water pH should be 7.0.

13. If the water is chlorinated, allow the water to stand for 24 hours. This will allow the chlorine from the water to dissipate. Fishes do not thrive well in chlorinated water.

14. Place the preferred fishes into the tank. When starting an aquaponics system, stock lightly. There should be a maximum of ½ inch of fish for each gallon of water in the tank. Allow the system to establish for about a month before increasing the density of fishes to 1 inch for every gallon.

15. Do not add plants immediately upon set up. Wait for about 4 weeks before adding plants to the aquaponics system.

Chapter 7:

Fish and Plants

There are many types of fishes and plants that can be grown and raised in an aquaponics system. These grow relatively faster, with higher yields and better qualities within a shorter period compared to traditional soil-grown plants and pond-raised fishes. In fact, in an 8 meters by 4 meters growing area, about 50 kilograms of fishes can be produced and hundreds of kilos of vegetables, all within only six months.

Choosing fishes

Choosing species depends on a few factors, however. First, you should consider the size of the tank. A smaller tank is only for fishes that grow small through adulthood. For instance, small goldfishes would be appropriate for a small fish tank. For larger species like carp and salmon, a larger container would be needed. Also, consider the natural growing conditions of the fishes. Tropical fishes can still be grown in colder regions, but the system would need a water heater.

Hobby fishes that are inedible and edible fishes can both be grown in aquaponics. The most common and successfully raised fishes in aquaponics include the following:

- Koi
- Oscars
- Tilapia
- Perch -   Catfish
- Goldfish
- Prawns (freshwater variety)
- Other varieties of aquarium fishes
- Peruvian Pacu

Choosing plants

Any type of plant can be grown using aquaponics. They will grow larger and yield more crops than with other farming methods. Some of the best plants to grow in aquaponics include the following:

Different lettuce varieties, such as iceberg and Romaine

Different kinds of herbs such as mint, basil, and rosemary

- Tomatoes

- Melons

- Cucumbers

- Watercress

- Zucchini

- Broccoli

- Squash
- Peppers

- Strawberries

Fish Food

This is an essential part of the system. As mentioned above, the fish food is what provides the plants with the different nutrients. You can either buy it from outside or you may choose to plant duckweed and grow worms.

There are two very simple techniques that you can use when foraging for fish food. This section covers the same.

Cultivating Duckweed

This is an extremely simple technique. You will have to cultivate and raise the duckweed in a large barrel. Make sure that you fill the barrel only to half its actual size. If you have the right conditions set, you will find that the duckweed has doubled itself within 24 hours! That is brilliant is it not? The optimum conditions are –

1. The temperature of the water must be between 60 – 70 degrees Fahrenheit.

2. The water must be filled with nutrients. These nutrients are obtained through the manure that is made out of donkey dung.

When you give your fish food that you have purchased from the market, you will find that the food has been gobbled up by the fish within the hour. You have to ensure that this does not happen. The fish consume duckweed slower than the commercial food. They take a minimum of 24 hours to eat up all the duckweed that has been provided to them. If you find that your fish have not consumed the duckweed from the previous day, you will only have to add a little more. The advantage with duckweed is that it only floats over the surface. The other advantageous factor is that it does not produce nitrate compounds like the commercial feed. The duckweed will be eaten and while it is floating on the surface, it continues to make more!

In a virtual world, this plant is active metabolically and can always be used as food for the fish or food in general. It has high concentrations of the essential nutrients and acids like lysine, amino acids, xanthophyll (which is a pigment found in plants), carotene (another pigment found in plants to give the plant color) and trace minerals. These nutrients and compounds make duckweed one of the best animal feeds for fish, goats and even cattle! You can be assured that there is no loss of nutrients if the duckweed is fed to the animals wet or dry.

You have read about how duckweed is good for different animals. Here's the catch. Duckweed needs to be provided nutrition to ensure that it grows or multiplies. What is the best food for duckweed? Nitrogen Ammonium! You do not have to go in search of this compound since the aquaponic system produces this material in abundance. But the trace minerals in duckweed are lacking since the aquaponic system works without soil. This means that both the fish and the plants lack these trace minerals. This can be overcome by adding evaporated sea salt to the system. This will be covered later.

Worm Composting

This is the second type of food that is easily available for the fish. This is done through the ancient culture of raising worms through the process of vermiculture. The advantage is that these worms like the duckweed, multiply or double very easily under the right conditions. Worms love moisture and the darkness. They also like to be given something to eat. These worms can be provided to fish as their feed and can also be consumed by human beings. They have a great nutritional content. A worm has 19% protein, 14% fat, 4% carbohydrates, 2% fiber and 63% moisture.

Worms to use

You cannot use all worms to feed the fish since every worm requires different conditions, which you may or may not be able to provide. The earthworms are the best bet! There are three categories of earthworms – deep burrowing, shallow dwelling, and little dwelling worms.

The deep burrowing worms can be compared to night crawlers. They need burrows that are drowned in darkness and have minimal disturbances. They live in these burrows with ease and can reproduce faster in these conditions. The shallow dwelling worms do not have their very own burrow. They keep moving through the first twelve inches of the soil. The litter dwellers are true to their name. They live in the litter that is commonly found on the top layer of the soil. Of these worms, the litter dwellers are the best worms to use for composting. If you have a pound of these worms, you will find that they have doubled just by converting a pound of scrap into compost.

Constructing a worm bin

To ensure that your worms have the best conditions, you will need to create a worm bin. This makes it easier for you as well. You would not want to forage through the soil in search of your worms. You will need to have a large plastic container or you can use a large wooden container. You will need different cloth – hardware and ground cloth. These have to be cut to fit the top of the container. You will need a wire mesh, some newspaper, and cardboard as well. Make sure that you do not use the glossy paper.

1. Drill holes in the container around the bottom to ensure that there is sufficient flow of air. Make sure that the holes are not wider than half an inch.

2. Then place the foam scraps at the bottom of the container. These foam scraps are very important for the composting of worms. There may be liquids that have been accumulated at the bottom of the container. These foam scraps absorb this liquid. This way you will not have to add an additional tray at the bottom of the container.

3. Identify the length of the container and cut the wire mesh to fit the container. Make sure that the wire mesh is cut so that it is 3 inches wider than the width of the container. It can be wider than that as well.

4. Fold the wire along the long edges to forms a stack. This way you will be able to ensure that the wire does not touch the bottom of the container. This allows the free flow of air in the container.

5. Take the ground cloth and the screen. You have to cut them so that they will fit your mesh wire perfectly. This will make sure that the bed that you have created does not dismantle easily.

6. You will now have to shred the newspaper into long strips. Make sure that the width is not too much.

7. Next cut the cardboard into tiny pieces that will be managed easily.

8. Soak the paper in water for a few minutes. Make sure that you do not soak them for so long that they tear into pieces on being brought out of the water. When you pull the paper out, it should feel like a sponge that had been dampened. When you squeeze the paper, the water should not drip from the paper.

9. Ensure that the worm container is filled with the damp paper. This

paper must be distributed evenly. It is best to fluff the papers out before you put them into the container since this allows for better air circulation.

10. Now that you have created the perfect environment for the worms, you should place the worms in the middle of the bedding. Make sure that you do not spread them over the entire surface of the bedding.

11. Cover the bin with a surface and make sure that the temperature lies between 59 – 77 degrees Fahrenheit.

Feeding your worms

You have talked about using the worms as food for your fish and sometimes for yourself. But what food do you have to provide to these worms? Have you thought about that? Once you have created your very own bin for the worms, you will have to give them time to adjust to their new surroundings. After a couple of days, you can bury some food in the bedding. You will have to ensure that you cover the food under tow inches of the bedding. This ensures that there is no smell that is emanating from the container. You will also be able to keep pests at bay. You can give the worms in the container vegetable and fruit scraps, tea and coffee bags and any cooked food as well. You should not give them any food with dairy products in them. Start with small quantities and increase the quantities slowly. Do not provide the worms with an extravagant amount of food instantly.

Harvesting your worms

The next step is to harvest your worms. When you find that the bedding in the container has reduced by half, you will have to add a piece of the screen to the bin. This screen has to be large to fit the top of the bin and cover the sides of the bin. You will find that the lid on the screen will hold it in place. You will have to fill the screen with the bedding and begin to provide food to the worms at the top of the bedding. You will then find the worms crawling right to the top of the screen. This is where the food is kept.

You will find that in two months, the worms should have crawled to the top most level. You will have to pick them out carefully and remove any of the castings that the worms leave at the bottom of the container. You will have to remove all the other contents of the container. Make sure that you separate the worms from the contents. You will have to remove all the bedding. Again add food for the worms at the top of the container. The worms will then move to where the new food is.

How to increase the trace nutrients in the system

As mentioned above, there are times when there are very few trace nutrients found in the aquaponic system. This can be overcome by adding evaporated sea salt to the system. There are so many lands that have become arable due to the accumulation of salt. Over 30% of the land that can be irrigated has become arable in most of the countries due to the accumulation of salts. It has been said that the plants – fruits and vegetables – should not have too much of salt. This means that the water in the area around the roots of the fruits and the vegetables should not have too much of salt in it. This is true! But there are certain salts that every plant requires. In every aquaponic system, the water passes through the system. However, it does not accumulate like it does in the soil in traditional soil gardening. If you consume 4 spoons of regular salt, you will die within the next twenty minutes. But this does not happen when sea salt is used. It may only lower the blood pressure in your body. This is not acceptable therefore you must not try this ever!

You will find that the average seawater has the same properties that blood does. It is a fact that seawater was used as a substitute for human blood in World War II. A drop of seawater contains the same amount of trace nutrients that regular human blood does. But there is a difference by a molecule or two.

It is a known fact that if there is a huge buildup of salt in the soil, there will be adverse effects on the growth of the plants. But it has been seen that the salinity of the water in parts per million in an aquaponics system can be high. Therefore, an aquaponics system can be used to meet the need of food all across the world. You can add one gallon of seawater to your system either once or twice a month. You will notice that your plants have begun to bloom and that the vegetables and fruits are vibrant and bright. You will find that both the fish and the plants in the system are healthier than before.

You will find a difference in the health because the water, which now contains the required nutrients, will pass through the gravel and will not build up like it does in the traditional soil gardening method. The plants that are in the system only absorb the nutrients that they require. Another reason why there is a sudden boost in the health of the plants is that the evaporated salt water helps in providing the roots with pure water that will enable the energy in the plant to be distributed evenly throughout the plant. In traditional soil gardening, the temperature of the soil plays a major role in determining the flow of energy in the plants.

You have to remember that the increase in the salinity of the water directly affects the amount of dissolved oxygen in the water. If there is an increase in the salinity, there will be a decrease in the dissolved oxygen. This implies that you have to ensure that the aeration is very high in this system. This helps you obtain large amounts of oxygen, which will benefit the plants and the fish in the system. You have to ensure that the pump in your system functions well since this ensures that there is enough dissolved oxygen in the system.

Chapter 8:

Problems and Solutions

Some problems may arise when maintaining an aquaponics system. There are a few common mistakes that some growers, especially beginners, make. These can spell trouble and incur losses in both fishes and plants. Here are the most common ones:

Bug problems

Most growers are not aware that even in aquaponics, bugs can still get to the plants. This is most especially so when the system is set up outdoors. Birds, too, may start pecking away at the fruits once these emerge. Insects and worms can destroy the foliage and may also damage fruits.

Ignoring bug problems can result in huge losses to a plant harvest. Growers cannot just spray the plants with pesticides and insecticides. These toxic chemicals will find their way into the fish tank and kill the fishes. One great solution is to turn a pest problem into a beneficial opportunity. Pick out the bugs, slugs, and caterpillars or use bug traps and drop them into the fish tank. These are welcome food for the fishes. The pest problem is controlled, and you'll save on fish food. A water spray would also work. This will dislodge any insects and worms that are feeding on the plants.

Tank Temperature

It is very important to consider the water temperature that the fishes normally thrive in. Most tropical fish varieties can withstand hot water temperatures.

Some fishes don't. Always check the optimum water temperature for the fishes and maintain them. Also, check for water temperature, PH and oxygenation when the fish tank is exposed outdoors in the summer heat. Hot water temperatures promote algae blooms and cause oxygen loss in the water. These can kill the fishes, so always check.

Testing Ammonia Levels

Not a lot of growers regularly check the levels of ammonia in the tank. Most often, there is the assumption that continuously flowing water is enough to keep ammonia levels in the fish tank low. Too much ammonia can actually kill the fishes. Check the ammonia regularly, at least once a week. There are many types of ammonia test kits that can be purchased and used.

Problems with worm composting

If you have begun to compost worms for fish feed, you may face the following problems.

These problems have been mentioned with the solutions making it easy for you to overcome these conditions. Your worm bin may have terrible odor. One of the main causes of this could be the fact that you have added too much food to the bin. As a solution, you must wait and add food to the bin only when you find that the last batch of food is almost over. You have to ensure that the food is covered under two inches of bedding. This always ensures that there are not too many flies around the bin.

There may be times when there is too much moisture in the worm container. This reduces the oxygen levels in the container. To remove the excess moisture, you can add more dry paper to the bedding. Mix the paper and fluff it out. This will ensure that there is more oxygen that is added to the system. You have to avoid placing meat and dairy products in the bin since they go rancid very quickly. If the worms find the conditions of the bin to be unfavorable, they will try to crawl out of the bin. You will have to ensure that there is light above the bin so that the worms do not crawl out. Constantly check the moisture in the bin and also change the bedding if required.

Chapter 9:

Your Very Own Start – Up Checklist!

As a beginner, you may want to take up a system design that is complicated. You forget, in your excitement, that you need to start slowly. Nobody becomes an expert in a minute. You may have heard the quote that Rome was not built in a day! That is what has to be followed while you are constructing your very own aquaponics system.

Size of the system

Before you begin working on the system, you have to decide which type of system you want to use and what the size of the system is going to be. You do not want a system that is difficult for you to handle. Start out small.

Conduct thorough research

You will have to zero in on a type of system and come up with the perfect design for your system. You will have to draw rough sketches and see what works best in your backyard. Once you have worked on the design, make a list of all the different parts that you will need. Then list out the stores and warehouses that you need to target to set up the system.

Purchase and assemble

You have to ensure that you do not spend too much when you are buying the products. When you have procured the parts of the system, you should begin assembling it in the way the parts look in your design.

Plants!

When you have finished assembling the system, try to see what plants you can sow in the system that you have assembled. Once you have made a list, you can see where you can obtain the seeds and where you can obtain the seedlings otherwise.

Circulation of water

Once you have assembled the part, you will have to enter the water into the system. Make sure that the water is filtered on a regular basis in the first few weeks after the system has been set up.

Watch your plants grow

You will now have to sow the seeds to your plants or put the seedlings in the system. Watch them grow! They are not going to shoot up like the Beanstalk in the fairy tale 'Jack and the Beanstalk'. They will take their time to grow.

Start nitrification

Since you have not entered the fish yet into the system, you will have to insert nitrifying bacteria into the system to ensure that the process of nitrification is happening easily. If there is an accumulation of ammonium in the water, you will find that the plants have begun to die or wither.

Add fish

You will now have to add the fish. You have checked the water filtering and have also seen how the process of nitrification works. In your fish rearing tanks, release the fish that you would like to use. Make sure that you are not using fish that will only soak up the nutrients. The fish in general release waste that contains numerous nutrients that the plants require.

Maintain the system

Every system, no matter how sound, will need maintenance on a regular basis. There are many parts in the system that needs to be monitored. You will have to check the quality of the water and maintain the pH of the system. A high or a low pH affects the nitrification process thereby killing both the fish and the plants. You will have to check the filters and the pump on a regular basis. You need to ensure that the pipes have not been clogged by the waste that is produced through the system.

How to manage the system

This section covers the few basic points that you will have to remember when it comes to the maintenance of the system.

1. You will have to feed the fish daily. You can buy commercial food or you can cultivate duckweed and grow worms at home to ensure that they grow well.

2. You will have to check the health of the fish daily. There is a possibility that the growth of some fish could be stunted. This fish would cause deterioration in the entire system. You will find that your plants have started to grow slowly or have started to produce fruits and vegetables that are not up to the mark. This is because the stunted fish is consuming all the essential nutrients.

3. You will have to test the water quality on a regular basis. In the first

few months, you will have to check the quality every two days. Once the system has matured, you can check the water quality once every month.

4. You will need to clean the system continuously. You will have to clean the pipes importantly. If the pipes are clogged, there will not be enough nutrients that are reaching the plants. The water may also stop flowing through the entire system, which will lead to the failure of the system. You have to clean the filters and ensure that the waste of the fish does not cause too much damage to the system. The food that is provided to the fish must also be removed on a regular basis. Food that is decomposing would require tons of oxygen. This would reduce the amount of dissolved oxygen in the water.

5. You will have to cut the plants and trim them. They have to be groomed on a regular basis.

6. Always keep an eye out for any bugs in the system

Grooming of plants

Many gardeners are afraid when it comes to grooming their container plants. One must remember that grooming helps the plant avoid pests and diseases.

There are four methods of grooming plants:

Pinching

Using your finger and thumb to cut a part of the stem is called 'Pinching.' This method helps in keeping the plants compact and also helps to retain the bushy shape of the plants. Remember to always pinch above the node. Pinching is usually advised for soft-stemmed plants.

If the plants cannot be pinched, use pruners to achieve the same.

Pruning

You must use pruning shears to trim plants with thick or woody stems. Remember to remove the parts of the plant that have been injured or have dried up in order to avoid the formation of fungus and diseases. Always remember to prune plants while they are rapidly growing, usually in spring or summer.

Deadheading Flowers

Always cut off dead or dry flowers, as they usually tend to attract gray mold, a fungus, which spreads diseases.

Cleaning

Always keep the plants clean. If the leaves are clean and dust free, they will attract enough sunlight and will grow boisterously. You can clean smooth leaves using a damp sponge; rough leaves using a soft brush and ferns using a water spray.

Tips and Tricks that come in Handy

This section covers the tips and tricks that come in handy when you are working on an aquaponics system in your very own backyard. You may have been overwhelmed by looking at the different aspects that you will have to consider. But do not worry! It is a simple process to follow if you put your mind to it!

1. You have to wash the gravel before you put it into the system. Gravel is usually dirty and will dirty the water in the entire system if not washed properly.

2. When you are looking at using different gravel media, compare them on the basis of their pH. You do not want to have any part of the system causing a fluctuation in the level of the pH. This is an important factor to consider.

3. There may be chlorine in the water that you are using. You can use Vitamin C or use an air pump to

bubble out the excess chlorine that is there in the tap water.

4. You can use worms to feed the fish. These worms, especially the red wigglers, are perfect for the system. They ensure that there is no area in the system that is anaerobic.

5. Always use products that are eco – friendly. Do not use any product that is full of chemicals. This only brings the system down!

6. If you find that there are pests on your plants, particularly aphids,
create a solution with vinegar and water, which can be sprayed on the plants.

7. You will have to ensure that there is no algae that is formed in the fish rearing tanks. You will need to ensure that the tanks are covered. If there is even a little sunlight entering

the tanks, algae will be formed. These algae will harm the fish and the entire system.

8. Never empty the entire system of its water. Only remove a third of the water every time you have to clean the system. If you empty out the entire water, you are destroying all the good bacteria that is found in the water.

9. If you have plants in the outdoors, give them good protection from the weather.

10. Your pumps work on electricity. If there is a shutdown of power, your entire system comes to a standstill. You will have to find alternative sources of power for your system.

Conclusion

Thank you again for purchasing this book!

I hope this book was able to help you to understand what aquaponics is, how it works, and how to set up your own aquaponics garden.

The next step is to look for a good location and start planning and setting up an aquaponics system of your own. Soon, you will be harvesting both plants and fishes in hauls. Your plants will be your reward. You can use the vegetables and fruits that you produce from the system in your daily cooking. If you think you can make a business out of selling the produce, go for it! Remember to harvest the produce every season since you will be able to use it for the future. Also remember to take care of your fish. Do not let them go hungry!

Thank you and

good luck!

CPSIA information can be obtained
at www.ICGtesting.com
Printed in the USA
BVHW040048270621
610451BV00006B/1535